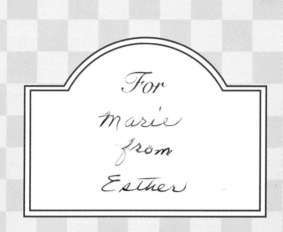

For
Marie
from
Esther

A Woman's Companion

SIMPLE GIFTS,
ABUNDANT
TREASURES

by
Beth Mende Conny

Illustrated by
Mullen & Katz

PETER PAUPER PRESS, INC.
WHITE PLAINS, NEW YORK

The quilt block on the front cover
is from a hand-designed pattern by
Katy Ball. For more information
about Katy Ball and her hand-made
quilted cards, contact:
The Quilted Cupboard, P.O. Box 6062,
Titusville, FL 32782.

Cover and book design by Mullen & Katz

To my daughters, Julia and Jenna,
who make my life so abundant

A Woman's Companion

SIMPLE GIFTS,
ABUNDANT
TREASURES

You race from moment to moment, place to place. And as you dash through your days, you think: "If I could only work smarter, faster, I'd be able to catch up with bills, housework, life. I'd be able to spend quality time with loved ones, return to school, get in shape, travel, write . . . enjoy myself."

Will this day ever come? The answer, quite simply, is "no." And that's a cause for celebration. For when you let go of the illusion that peace, happiness, and relaxation are contingent on having all loose ends tied into neat bows, you take a giant leap toward living the life you've always wanted and deserved—a *life full of simple gifts and abundant treasures.*

This book will help you discover in simple, gentle ways that there is nothing you must first do or become to live the Good Life. All you need is a willingness to stop, look, and listen to the person within who truly knows what she wants, needs, and loves.

Through the daily meditations that follow, the woman within will become your guardian angel, conscience, guide. Together, you will examine the truly important issues in your life and cast off those that are trivial. You will become lifelong friends who embrace each day as a gift to be treasured and who discover the simple pleasures that previously seemed so out of reach.

In the process, your heart will open and respond not just to the beauty in your life but to the beauty of life itself—a life full of wonderful people and places, and profound lessons.

B. M. C.

TO BEGIN ANEW,
YOU MUST OPEN ONE DOOR
WHILE CLOSING ANOTHER

Perhaps what's so difficult about beginning something new is having to turn from the old. Just as you can fit only so much water in a glass, so too can you fit only so many old ways of thinking, doing, and being in your life.

You must be willing to welcome change by creating space for it. For some women, creating space means casting off old clothes and papers, unhealthy relationships and negative thought patterns. For others, the process is more subtle: they simply decide they can no longer carry on with business as usual.

Whatever your preference or style, all you ultimately need is a willingness—however faint—to live a more enriching life. This willingness opens the door unto a new world filled with abundant treasures.

**REAL CHANGE
BEGINS
NOT WITH
GOALS AND
ACHIEVEMENTS
BUT WITH
ACCEPTANCE**

Okay, you say, you're ready and willing, but are you able to allow change in your life? How many times have you promised yourself or proclaimed to others that you were going to get your life together—lose those stubborn pounds, switch jobs or mates, start saving—only to snap back like a rubber band stretched too far? Why should you succeed now when you've failed to achieve lasting change before?

Because, now, the change you're seeking is not dependent on your achieving a particular goal or radically altering your personality. Rather, it has at its heart acceptance of the unique person you are, here, now.

Love and accept your true self—strengths, shortcomings, and all—and you develop a new outlook on life. You begin to differentiate between what's important and not, acceptable and not. You also begin to identify what you absolutely *must* do to live a life of integrity, purpose, and joy. Then, and only then, is lifelong change possible.

CONSULT YOUR INNER COMPASS AND YOU'LL ALWAYS FIND YOUR WAY

To move your life in the right direction, you need a sense of direction, a sense of what you want and need. Wouldn't it be nice to have a magical compass to help you find your way, to indicate when you're on track or off course? Well, you do: your heart.

Your heart knows when you are in sync with your dreams or straying too far from them, when you are living authentically or in accordance with someone else's plans.

Let the compass within guide you toward the life you deserve. As you go about your daily activities, ask yourself—"Is this what I should be doing?" "Is this what I want?" Let your heart respond. Its answers will surprise you.

LET THE WHISPERS OF YOUR SOUL SHOUT TO YOU

The kids scream, the TV blares, the telephone rings, the dog howls. . . . Welcome to everyday life, where noise surrounds you like the very air you breathe.

How in all this boisterous chaos do you hear the murmurs of your heart? The trick is not to quiet the world (an impossible task at best!) but to quiet yourself.

No, you don't have to run off and meditate or lock yourself in a soundproof room. Rather, pause for a moment, take a few deep breaths, and listen to the sounds that cannot be heard. Listen to the longings of your heart.

When you pause to turn your attention within, the whispers of your soul shout to you, letting you know what you should be doing.

Today, in the middle of your hectic schedule, stop occasionally to hear what only you can hear— the sounds of truth.

TO GET THE RIGHT ANSWER, YOU MUST ASK THE RIGHT QUESTION

Sometimes we're so intent on finding answers that we forget the importance of questions.

The questions we ask and the way in which we ask them frame the responses we receive. Phrase questions in positive ways that inspire the mind to think along new lines, and you get answers that provoke excitement and action.

For example, instead of asking, "When will I ever enjoy my life?" ask, "What one enjoyable thing can I do for myself today?" Turn questions like, "Why am I such a failure?" into "What three things am I good at, and how can I build on these strengths for even greater success?"

Starting today, use your words to your advantage. Make them upbeat, dynamic, reflective of your new and improved approach to life.

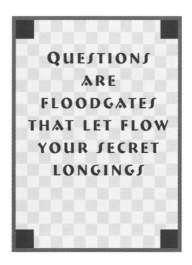

QUESTIONS ARE FLOODGATES THAT LET FLOW YOUR SECRET LONGINGS

Depending on how they're phrased, questions can empower or disempower, open doors, or slam them shut. Questions have other powers as well: they help reveal your deepest wishes and desires.

To illustrate, get a paper and pen and answer the following questions, allowing no more than two minutes for each. Don't worry about grammar, spelling, or what someone else might say. Just keep your hand moving.

What childhood friend
would you like to see again, and why?

What 25 things
would you like to have accomplished
by the time you're 80?

You've just been named
person of the year by *Time* magazine.
What is your accomplishment?

What do your answers reveal about your aspirations and needs? What other questions can you ask to awaken your sleeping dreams?

Commit to asking yourself a provocative question each day. Take note of your answers. Over time, they will become stepping stones to the life you love.

TO LIVE A LIFE YOU LOVE, YOU MUST KNOW WHAT YOU LOVE

You want to love your life, yet you've lost touch with what you love. That's easy to understand, given the many hats you wear each day and how you often put the needs of others before your own.

The time has come, however, to re-establish contact with the things that engage and nurture you. It's time to fall in love again.

But where do you begin? Do you even remember what you enjoy or what makes you feel alive?

Don't worry, it will come back to you as easily as riding a bike. Just grab a pen and a lined sheet of paper, and on each line complete the sentence: "I love . . ." Work quickly to fill the sheet, jotting down whatever comes to mind, no matter how trivial or silly. For love comes in all shapes and sizes, and when you recognize its many forms, you begin to understand how its embers will fire your enthusiasm and warm your heart and days.

EVERY DAY
IS FILLED WITH GIFTS
WE GIVE OURSELVES

What do you love? chocolate? romance novels? movies that make you cry? the feel of your child's hand in yours?

Chances are you could fill not one but several pages with things you love to do, share, and experience. Happily and with few exceptions, the majority of them require no great commitment of time or money. In other words, they're simple gifts you can give yourself *today*—and every day.

Look over your list and choose one gift to enjoy today. Buy yourself flowers . . . go shopping with a friend . . . fix a candlelit dinner—you get the idea. Tomorrow, choose another gift and another the day after that. Before you know it, your life will be filled with abundant treasures. Each day will become an opportunity to express and embrace love and to spread its rays on others.

DREAMS ARE GOALS THAT YOU COMMIT TO ACT UPON

Love is the soil that helps you establish healthy roots. Goals are the rays of sun that allow you to break through the earth and reach toward the stars.

Not all goals are worthy of your time or effort, however. Some take you where you've already been; others have been set by those you want to please; still others have lost their relevancy, becoming hollow, even trivial, over the years.

Goals should not be set as much as chosen— with care and respect for who you are and what you value. Goals that reflect your true wants, needs, and aspirations are the goals you will accomplish. They are the dreams you make real in an awakened life.

A GOAL IS A GAUGE
THAT MEASURES
YOUR SUCCESS—
AND ENJOYMENT

Like road signs, goals guide you through life's journeys. Some goals, however, appear so distant as to be unobtainable. How do you reach them?

Step by step, yard by yard. There's no other way.

That's why it's essential to set interim goals. Like mile markers, they help you gauge how far you've come. They also provide turnoffs and overlooks that allow you to relax and reflect on where you've been and where you've yet to go.

More important, they help you enjoy the journey. Each marker adds to your sense of accomplishment and increases your confidence and enjoyment of life.

What interim goals can *you* set on the way to achieving your larger dreams?

DON'T WORK HARDER—
WORK SOFTER

All roads have their bumps, curves, and detours. That's life. Often, however, what you view as a setback is merely a temporary stall. The universe is telling you to stop, reconsider, rest. Perhaps it is time to fill your tank with new thoughts, people, activities. Maybe you need to overhaul your engine by eating more healthfully, exercising regularly, or embracing a more positive attitude.

Whatever the case, use this time as an opportunity to take a deep breath and regroup. Now is not the time to work harder but softer, to go with the flow and enjoy the ride. Sooner than you expect, you'll be on the road again, more confident than ever behind the wheel.

USE STYLE AS A MIRROR TO REFLECT WHO YOU ARE

As you embark on life's journeys, why not travel in style?

Style is a mirror that reflects the diverse aspects of your being. These reflections are evident in the way you dress, speak, and carry yourself; in your choice of books, paintings, and music; and even in the objects and people with which you surround yourself.

But are these reflections accurate? Do they represent the real you or the person you long to become?

Reflect on these reflections. Gently consider the colors and people you are drawn to, the fabrics and furniture that make you feel comfortable, the types of music and literature that speak to your soul.

Find ways to more fully incorporate your preferences into your everyday life. Wrap a colorful scarf around your waist, wear a pair of wild earrings to work, luxuriate in your favorite chair while listening to your favorite piece of music. . . . Let the world know who you truly are!

UNCOVER
THE REAL YOU—
WITH CLOTHES
THAT CELEBRATE
YOUR
DISTINCTIVE
STYLE

Do your clothes reveal or disguise the real you? Let's go to your closet and find out.

Take a quick inventory, rating each piece of clothing on a scale from 1 to 10. Let 1 represent articles you rarely wear because they're too worn, out-of-date, or uncomfortable. Let 10 represent items you wear often because they're beautifully designed, timelessly styled, and make you feel like a million bucks.

Give away all clothes that fall in the 1 to 4
range—let those who like or could use them enjoy
their wear. Hang onto clothes in the 5 to 7 range,
at least for now. Many of these items can be given
a facelift with the help of distinctive accessories or
minor alterations. The rest can be phased out as
time and money allow.

And what of the clothes in the 8 to 10 range?
Study them to determine what makes them winners.
Is it their color or weave, their ease of care or
simple design, their ability to mix and match? Use
them as standards for developing, even flaunting,
your distinctive style.

MAKE YOUR HOME A CASTLE IN WHICH YOU HOUSE YOUR DREAMS

The space in which you live says a lot about how you live. Is your home your castle, reflecting your aesthetic values, or is it more like a giant storeroom, bursting with clutter and clashing furniture?

How do you transform your living space into breathing space—an environment that, like a deep inhalation, soothes your soul?

You begin as you did with your clothes, by evaluating what you own and how well it reflects who you are. Next, you sharpen your sights by homing in on the colors, patterns, materials, and styles that speak to you. Browse shops and magazines and take special note of inviting interiors, be they storefronts, restaurants, or friends' apartments. Create a file for ideas, paint swatches, fabric samples.

Let these visual cues seep in and, gently, over time, they will lead you like an experienced guide to your destination: a living space that truly supports your values and being.

THINK
SMALL,
THINK
SACRED

Redecorating is great, you say, but who has the time, money, or even energy for such a big project?

There's no need to think big. In fact, you'd do better to think small and to begin by creating your own sacred space.

What is a sacred space? It could be a room or a corner of one, a special chair or bookcase, a

closet or a windowsill. Whatever its dimensions, it's an area of your home that is yours and yours alone to adorn with furniture or objects that are beautiful and significant.

Think of this sacred space as a talisman that you touch visually and which connects you to the woman within. This is the space to which you come to center yourself, to remind yourself of what is important. Full of fresh flowers, bright colors and prints, heartwarming photographs, comfortable pillows, favorite books—you decide—it awaits you at the start and end of each day, whenever you need a refuge.

Let your eyes wander across the landscape of your home and find a space to consecrate. Sanctify it with meaningful belongings, soothing thoughts . . . love.

EMBRACE
YOUR
"LIFE" STYLE

Just as you have your own style in clothes and furnishings, so too do you have a style for navigating life's changes. Know and accept your style and you increase your ability to move comfortably in new directions.

Often, however, the grass seems greener and the road smoother when you watch others progress. And you think, "If only I were like him or her—

more daring/thoughtful/willing/open. I could
turn my life around in no time."

But what works for one person doesn't
necessarily work for another. Ultimately, you
must follow your own path, propelled by your
own energy.

Learn from the experiences and insights of
others, but learn from yourself as well. Think of
changes you have made in the past, goals reached,
dreams realized, however large or small. What do
they tell you about the way you perceive and act
upon the world? How can you use your personal
style as a tool to better shape your authentic self?

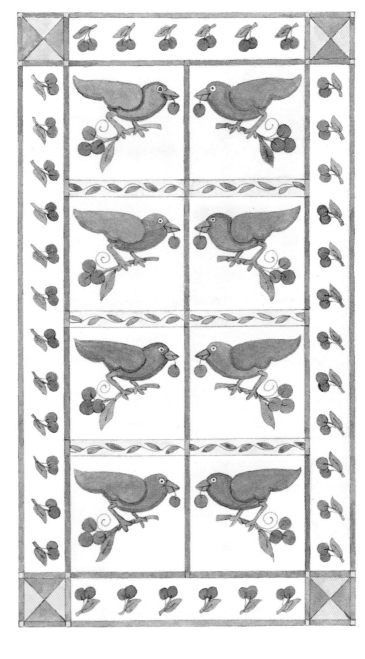

SMALL STEPS, GIANT LEAPS

Like most people, you want to do great things in life, take giant leaps forward. And you can—if you're willing to take smaller steps as well. Ultimately, the length of your stride doesn't matter. Getting where you want to go is what's important.

Small steps over time add up to great leaps. Each leads you to—and prepares you for—the next.

Celebrate each step you make, no matter how big or small. Know that each will lead you closer, closer, closer still to your dreams.

MAKE FRIENDS
WITH FAITH

Discover the companion who will always be there for you when times get rough: faith.

Faith is a friend who knows and loves the real you. She is there to help you reach your dreams and overcome whatever obstacles stand in your way. She can see beyond the next hill, around the next corner, past the next challenge. She knows that if you persevere, nothing can stop you; you will have what you want and be who you'd like.

And what does this friend ask in return? Just one thing: that you believe in her.

Believe in the power of faith and you learn to believe in yourself; you learn to believe in the rightness of your dreams and the path you have set out upon. No longer do you journey alone. You have a friend at your side who will gladly take your hand in hers.

DAY 19

THINK POSITIVELY
ABOUT
NEGATIVE THINKING

You want to be a positive thinker, yet negative thoughts seep into your consciousness. Before you know it, you're thinking of all sorts of worst-case scenarios.

Well, don't stop there! Rather, make each scenario as real and specific as possible. In other words, name your fears: "I won't get a raise." "I won't lose 15 pounds." "I'll never publish my novel."

Now, for the magical next step. Think of positive ways to overcome each situation: "I'll get off my duff and look for a new, more exciting job at a great salary." "I'll buy clothes that make me look beautiful now, instead of waiting until I reach my ideal weight." "I'll join a writer's group for support and constructive criticism." Get the idea?

Use this exercise to bring your dark thoughts into the light and in no time at all you'll be able to turn your worst-case scenarios into golden opportunities.

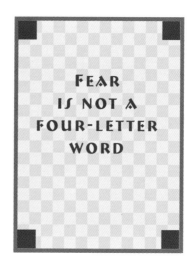

FEAR
IS NOT A
FOUR-LETTER
WORD

Most people treat fear like a four-letter word that should be banished from their vocabularies. Fear, however, has its place, and an important one at that.

Often, fear is a sign that you are moving too far, too fast. The pit in your stomach warns you to slow down, weigh your options, develop a more realistic plan of action.

Fear also is a placemark that notes where your pockets of resistance lie. Procrastination, spinning your wheels, biting off more than you can chew— all are forms of resistance that put the brakes on your momentum, and each must be examined, even reasoned with, before you can move forward.

Fear is a natural response when you journey beyond the circle of your everyday life. Even the bravest of explorers show caution when they venture into uncharted territory. You should expect no less of yourself.

Rather than banish fears, try to dissipate them. Accept their presence and role in your life. Listen to what they are trying to tell you. Go within to form your response, then move past them with a smile and wave of thanks.

CONFIDENCE IJ AN
ACQUIRED TRAIT

Like walking, playing the piano, and baking a soufflé, confidence must be learned, then practiced.

At times this doesn't appear to be the case. You look around and note that some people seem to move through life without doubt or hesitation. Were they born that way?

No, but they have developed a track record of small and large achievements from which they've learned much about themselves and life. And they've parlayed this knowledge into stepping stones that place them firmly on the ground.

Whether you realize it or not, you are one of these people. You can prove it to yourself by getting a pen and paper and listing the areas in which you've established a track record. Next, identify the areas in which you'd like to set new records and build greater confidence.

Set your sights on the future, but don't lose sight of the present. It is in the here and now, in the daily act of practice, that you gain mastery.

ALL PRAYERS ARE ANSWERED, THOUGH NOT ALL IN THE WAY YOU EXPECT

Sometimes life makes other plans.

You set your goals, work diligently to achieve them, speak kindly of others, go to bed early, eat your vegetables, and still, you don't get where you want to go. It's not fair!

But it happens, and often it happens for the best, although it may not seem that way at the time. Truth is, life's greatest gifts frequently come wrapped in unanswered prayers.

With time and perspective, you realize that what you considered the only path was actually a dead end, what you considered an insurmountable obstacle was merely a stepping stone, what you considered a defeat was actually the beginning of a different kind of achievement.

Be patient, have faith. Learn to cherish the prayers life answers—directly and in surprising ways.

START
YOUR OWN
FAN CLUB

Wouldn't it be great if everyone appreciated your goodness and humor, recognized your talents and potential, encouraged your dreams, and respected your needs?

That's a lot to ask of others, but it's not too much to ask of yourself. For how you treat yourself sets the standard for how others will treat you.

Become your most devoted fan. Speak of yourself to others in positive ways. Use equally positive language in conversations with yourself. Be honest; be fair; most important, be loving. The battle is half won when you have yourself on your side.

EVERY DAY IS A VACATION IN THE HERE AND NOW

Today is a vacation day. Congratulations! You deserve it.

You've been working hard (and soft!) to set new goals and adopt a new, more positive outlook, and you've taken real and constructive steps to nurture your authentic self.

Today, however, the woman within wants the day off. She wants to put her feet up and enjoy the simple pleasures of life: the sunlight filtering through the trees, the smell of freshly baked cookies, the infectious laughter of her children and friends, the soft touch of the man she loves.

The woman within knows that life's great treasures can be had at any time—and that the time is *now*.

Enjoy today with her. Open the day's many gifts and embrace the abundance of your life. There is nothing you must do or become to live a rich, full life. You merely have to awaken your senses and let life's abundance flood in.

YOUR
BODY,
YOUR
FRIEND

Self-love is all-encompassing—it requires
that you love your body as well as your mind.

How often do you look in the mirror and
send your body loving thoughts? How often do you
thank it for always being there for you, from the
moment you rise to the moment you fall exhausted
into bed at night?

Your body is home to your thoughts, feelings, dreams. It is the vehicle through which you realize your goals. And it is a reflection of what you truly think of yourself.

Love your body as you would a best friend. She isn't perfect (who is?), but she is there to support and build your self-esteem. Be a good friend to her as well. Make sure she gets plenty of sleep and exercise and eats her greens. Dress her in outfits that accent her beauty and make you proud to be in her company.

As you catch her eye in the mirror, give her a heartfelt smile. Let her know you love her *as is* and that you're happy to have her share your life.

CLEAR,
PRUNE,
WEED . . .
DISCOVER
THE
ESSENTIAL

   Vacations are special times that help you
break free of everyday demands and routines. They
also give you time and space to nurture other parts
of yourself.

   How quickly these parts disappear once
you're back at home or work. And you wonder:
Where did that relaxed, clear-thinking, fun-loving
woman go?

Know that she's still with you, waiting to be invited into your busy life. To make room for her, you must begin the slow but important process of simplifying your life.

Think of the wildfires you normally put out during the day and the squeaky wheels you continually try to quiet. Are these efforts truly worth your time and energy? What can you cast off or delegate? What, with better planning, can you do less frequently?

Question your assumptions: Why *do* I have to go food shopping on the weekends? Why *must* I spend every holiday with relatives? Why *am* I volunteering on a project I care little about?

Like a gardener, learn to clear, prune, and weed. Your time is the valuable soil in which the woman within grows. Beginning today, let her enter your life and fully blossom.

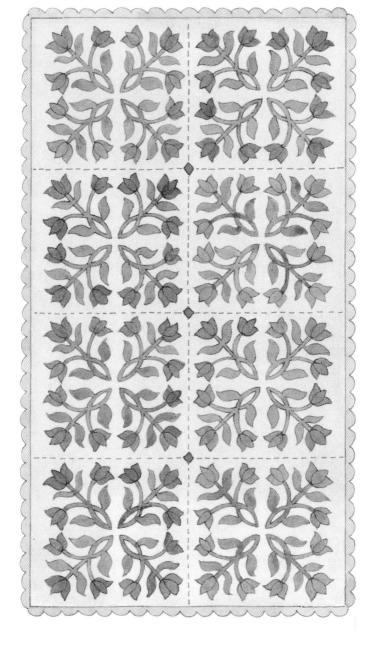

USE HINDSIGHT
TO GAIN FORESIGHT

Simplifying your life is anything but simple. That's why it's helpful to follow the Rocking Chair Rule.

The Rule works like this: Imagine you are 80, sitting on your porch in your rocking chair. As you rock, basking in the sunlight, surveying the distant, lush hills, think back on what was truly important in your life. What accomplishments are you most proud of? What people still bring a smile to your face? What places, adventures, and events are as meaningful now as they were then?

Now, bring yourself back to the present. Think of the deadlines you scramble to meet, the chores you struggle to keep up with, the routines you unquestionably follow. Will any of these matter later on, when you're 80?

If not, think of ways to cast them off or move them off center stage. Devote yourself instead to those things that have a lasting value,

those things that you'll remember with fondness decades from now.

Let the Rocking Chair Rule be your gauge for measuring the importance of your daily activities. In the process, you'll learn to simplify your life by focusing on what truly matters, now and always.

BEGIN A MEANINGFUL CORRESPONDENCE WITH YOUR BEST FRIEND—YOU!

Like the Rocking Chair Rule, journaling is another great way to identify what truly matters and communicate with the woman within. Each page becomes a sacred space for your thoughts, feelings, hopes, and dreams. And as your words take shape, so too does your life. For the act of writing affirms what you hold most dear and helps you act in ways that give each day meaning and purpose.

You can derive the benefits of keeping a journal in as little as 10 minutes a day, or in a single, longer weekly session. The key is to let your hand glide across the page, unencumbered by judgmental thoughts or concerns about good writing.

Imagine that you are a channel for the woman within. Let her speak softly, loudly, with humor and rage. Let her ramble, analyze, be herself. Let the depth of her wisdom guide your pen. Let the words you share create an unbreakable bond between you, a bond based on respect, love, and friendship.

FRIENDSHIP IS A TREASURE YOU GIVE AND RECEIVE

Friends are one of life's greatest treasures. They share your adventures, help calm your troubled waters, and are there when you need them with laughter and love.

Friends also give you the opportunity to move beyond yourself, to give of yourself and learn more of the ways of the world and the lives of others.

Not all friends are people, however. Great books, powerful music, long walks, favorite hobbies—all are good friends that not only entertain and comfort but inspire and support personal growth.

Seek out the company of dear friends and make them part of your everyday life. Note how their presence enriches and helps soften life's rougher edges, how they help you gain perspective and courage, and how, when you are with them, you are never alone.

Think, too, of your role as friend. How can you open your heart wider to make the world even brighter, sweeter, more comfy for those you love?

YOU ARE A
MAGICIAN
IN A MAGICAL
WORLD

Some days the world spins so madly that it's all you can do to hang on. On other, rarer, days, it moves gently, sweetly through the universe, giving you time to stop and appreciate its natural beauty. There's a rainbow arching across the horizon, a gentle breeze tickling your skin. The birds converse excitedly in the trees; the grass shimmers beneath a rising sun.

Is there magic in the air? Yes, but it's a magic that's always there. All you have to do is notice it.

Make a point of looking beyond the hustle and bustle of your everyday life to the magical world that surrounds you. Sunny skies; crisp, white snow; geraniums ablaze in a flower box; a lone acorn on the sidewalk—each is part of a greater whole, a whole to which you also belong.

Ponder the miracle of life, its astounding complexity and simple beauty. Find a vista, a plant, or even a photograph of a lovely landscape to study. Let your eyes wander across it, noting its colors and dimensions.

Consider that the "work of art" before you is just one, infinitesimally small part of the world's total beauty. Multiply that beauty a millionfold and you begin to call forth the magic that is at your fingertips.

Abracadabra! Make the magic yours.

YOU ARE BOTH
YOUR CREATOR
AND YOUR
MASTERPIECE

Life may be short, but its moments are long. Each is a fresh canvas on which you paint in bright colors and in vivid detail the masterpiece that is your life.

Be bold in your brush strokes. Experiment with shapes, styles, and textures. Create compositions that are balanced and intriguing and which reveal the sacredness of life. Your life.

Let each painting, each moment, reveal life's simple gifts and abundant treasures. Let each shine a light on your authentic self and reveal what you now know:

You are special. You are unique. You are one of life's wondrous creations.